WHILE RIVERS FLOW

WHILE RIVERS FLOW

SOPHIE G. MICHAELS

Artelune Publishing

While Rivers Flow

Published by Artelune Publishing
Tampa, Florida
For information on this book or any of our other titles, please contact the
Director of Sales at 407-209-6494.

ISBN 979-8-9896290-0-8
ISBN 979-8-9896290-1-5 (ebook)

10 9 8 7 6 5 4 3 2 1

First Artelune Trade Paperback Edition: May 2024

Printed in the United States of America

Thia book is a work of fiction. Any references to historical events, real people, or
real places are used fictitiously. Other names, characters, places, and events are
products of the author's imagination. Any resemblance to actual events, places, or
persons, living or dead, is entirely coincidental.

Works quoted in *While Rivers Flow* lie within the Public Domain:
"Song of Joan" by Christine de Pizan, 1429
"Sonnet XX" by Thomas Lodge, 1593
"The Seven Ages of Man" from *As You Like It* by William Shakespeare, 1599
"The Passionate Shepherd to His Love" by Christopher Marlowe, 1588
"High Flight" by John Gillespie Magee, Jr., 1941

For all who love, and especially for those whom I love most - Mom, Dad, Vivienne, the Jameses, Abby, John, Theresa, Mary, and the rest of my extensive family. Thank you for your love and support!

Contents

THE OTHER SIDE

4
LOVE AND WAR

5
TRUE LOVES

6
HIGHER LOVES

7
LOVE CONTINUES

A poem is a garden of words,
created to bring beauty to those who read it.

Preface

Poetry is said to be the highest form of literary expression. It can tell any story, express any emotion that prose can tell, but it is prose formed and shaped with the author's pen until it becomes a gem.

Or maybe it owes its shape not to the author's pen, but to the author's voice. Poetry has been with us since our earliest days, when a blind poet sang his tales for a good meal and a chance at immortality. Innumerable wandering poets have traded their words for a seat by the fire and a mugful of the local alcohol. Women wrote and performed poems, first to entertain themselves and the other women of the household, then for the whole house or even larger audiences.

Every human culture has its own poetic forms, some focused on syllable counts, some on the repetition of sounds or the rhythm of the words. Some made the use of poetic forms for basic communication a necessary skill for anyone hoping to be considered worthy of their social status. Can you imagine what it would be like if every email you wrote had to be a sonnet and every text message had to be a haiku? Children would learn to write five-stanza poems in preparation for writing every research paper of their college career in iambic pentameter. Or maybe we'd get by with a rhyming couplet whenever possible.

The poetic forms we know today probably started out as ways to make it easier to memorize the work – Homeric scholars point out several places where this is obviously the case – but they help make it more memorable than regular prose. This focus on sounds and rhythms requires a certain amount of wordsmithing, to make the words express everything the author intends while fitting into the chosen form. This pressure turns poetry into gemstones, or at least into semi-precious stones.

I can't say any of my works are better than garnets, but I've been inspired by some real diamonds. I grew up on Homer, Virgil, Tolkien, and Shakespeare, but it wasn't until I read the works of Marie de France and the other poets of the Middle Ages that I truly discovered my poetic voice. The literary renaissance of the twelfth century brought with it a flowering of romantic poetry that was unequaled by anything since the Roman Empire. And maybe I'd just read the wrong Roman poets, but none of them had written works that really resonated with me, aside from Virgil's unapproachably epic storytelling.

The poets of the medieval *fin amour* (generally translated to "courtly love") genre were different. They wrote of love in a way that was heart-felt and fresh, a way that made the effort they'd put into the work al-most invisible. And some of them, often the best of them, were female. This might have been a big reason why their works resonate with me, because a woman naturally expresses her love and desire for her lover in different ways than a man does. These poets inspired me to copy their voice and make it my own.

And yes, I've included a few poems where I didn't even attempt a medieval voice, though they're still in the theme of love. I can only hope that you will love them as much as I do.

Sophie G. Michaels

28 May 2023

I

Youthful Loves

A Sister's Lament

Phillippe! Phillippe, why do I know
That thou art dead and gone?
Why should my heart grow cold and still
When to my mind you come?

'Tis now three weeks since that awful dream –
I sat up in cold sweats.
You'd fallen, not from sword, or arrow like Michel,
But weakened from within.

Try as I might, I've shook it not,
This certain, knowing dread.
Our orchards, loaded as they are with flowers,
To me seem dead and grim.

My ladies – since then, their pleasant, pastime chatter
Hath seemed a drone-like hum.
My spindle, well, it drops for you
More often than it spins.

Care you not what this will to our Father do?
You were the eldest, heir!
My protector, my brother, and my friend,
Who will protect us now?

The guards outside call out; a messenger approaches.
Father will rush the gate as fast
As dignity and crippled leg allow,
Certain he'll hear of your swift return.

I'll not go down. I've no need to hear
From a stranger the dismal truth.
There – do you hear? Our father cries out!
How could you hurt him so?

* * *

The first medieval poem I ever wrote, "A Sister's Lament" is written from the point of view of a young woman who learns that the last of her older brothers has died during the Third Crusade. She grieves for him, but she also feels angry at him for adding to their father's pain.

The lines "My spindle, well, it drops for you / More often than it spins" are a reference to an old superstition I grew up hearing, that a hand spindle (used for spinning loose fibers into thread for weaving or sewing) will drop if someone close to the spinner dies. I've no idea how widespread or old this superstition might be, since I haven't found a clear reference to it anywhere. It does seem, though, to be based on the widespread imagery of the Three Fates, who spin, measure, and cut the threads of our lives and weave them into the tapestry of human history. And did you know that the ancient Greeks imagined Aphrodite using a spindle to create new lives?

Penelope's Gift

A sweet young maid sits at her loom,
"Whom shall I marry, Mother?"
The shuttle passes back and forth
Marrying warp to weft.
"Is he handsome and young, or wise and old?
Is he a father, while I am yet a maid?"

The maiden knows she'll marry soon.
"Whom shall I marry, Mother?"
The web she weaves she'll wear that day
As she stands there blushing shyly.
"Is he ugly but young, scarred in old age?
"Will his sons laugh that he weds a child?"

The quiet damsel whispers her fears,
"Whom shall I marry, Mother?"
To her mother and to her loom,
She utters her fears in trust.
"Is he drinker or braggart, old but not wise?
Is his girth of sinew or fat?"

Her mother is silent but weeps inside
"Whom shall I marry, Mother?"
As a daughter's fears revive
Her own from so long ago.
"Is he brave and gentle, true knight or brazen churl?
Will he love me true or beat me without mercy?"

The girl weaves well despite her doubts.
"Whom shall I marry, Mother?"
Doubt and fear can slow her not
As she weaves child into woman.
"Is he dull or brash, humble or wicked?
Will he provide, or waste his wealth and mine?"

The sweet young maid weaves at her loom.
"Whom shall I marry, Mother?"
While every even her mother returns
To do loving Penelope's work.
"Is he fine and manly, or oafish and cruel?
Whom shall I marry, Mother?"

* * *

I wrote "Penelope's Gift" after reading about a relatively unknown type of medieval poem called a *chanson de toile*, a genre of poems about women's lives that were apparently often recited or sung while women were doing their household work.

If you've read or watched Diana Gabaldon's *Outlander*, you saw a portrayal of a later type of chanson de toile in the scene where Claire is sent to help the men gathering the rents and finds her way to a table where a group of women are beating a length of wool cloth in urine while chanting a song with a steady beat. The song kept the women moving on the same beat and maybe made up for a bit of the smell so they could full the wool into a denser, more water-repellant fabric. Luckily, the urine would be aged, so the smell would be more like bottled ammonia than like... you know.

Those familiar with the classics might recognize the reference to Queen Penelope, Odysseus' wife, and realize that her gift is time. In this case, it is time for a child to grow into an adult before she faces adult issues like marriage.

The Festival was Over

The festival was over; all were making long farewells.
My own dear and most beloved aunt
Then gestured to you and declared, "boy, take me home."
And though I knew 'twas nothing to it
But fair and knightly service to a much-beloved lady,
I felt a pang of jealousy.
For I would be the one with rights to you,
And the rest I would take would be in your arms.

* * *

The social structure of noble households in medieval Europe means that a young lady such as the one in this poem would most likely know few young men other than the ones in service to her father or to the husband of the lady who is training her for her own adult role. This young lady's first love is a young knight in service to her aunt – or, more likely, to that aunt's husband.

Jealousy is a common trope in medieval courtly love and the poetry associated with it. Medieval writers seem to have considered it to be one of the signs that their love was real, because of course we only feel jealous if our love is real and someone appears to be threatening it. The girl envies her aunt's right to claim the young knight's service, even if she fantasizes having a different type of relationship with him than what her aunt presumably has.

The Girl Beside the Throne

You stand, so solemn, watching each one
Who would approach your Queen.
Each gesture that she makes, enough
To summon aught that she might want.

Her pale and quiet shadow,
A flower of Her court.
Do you have dreams of future days,
A king to call your own?

* * *

I recently saw a photograph of a young woman I know, who was standing beside the queen's throne at a medieval reenactment several years ago. The young woman was serving her queen with a solemnity that made me think about her and what lay ahead for her in the future.

Historically, the royals and nobles of the Middle Ages were most closely served by the children of their highest-ranking vassals and allies. In turn, the children were trained in all the skills they were expected to need for the roles they would one day fill, as a sort of on-the-job training. When it was time, the couple who had been entrusted with the youth or maiden would often be the ones deciding who to marry him or her off to, especially if they outranked the child's parents. After all, that was a big part of why the couple was entrusted with him or her in the first place, because higher-ranking nobles could arrange a more prestigious match.

A girl who serves as cupbearer and handmaiden to a queen would most likely be doing so in preparation for her own state marriage, perhaps even to a king. Who would not grow solemn thinking of her own future under those circumstances?

Summer

Blue water beckons,
Small fish glisten under waves,
A choice awaits.

Bright blooms drift like snow,
Leaves rustle in fragrant air,
Clouds darken above.

Hard winds break pink blooms,
Rivers flow down golden bells,
Air turns to water.

Drops gather on bells,
Petals sail on swollen streams,
Dogs wrestle below.

Dark clouds sail northward,
Sandals slip on muddy walks,
The sun emerges.

Waves below turn blue,
Gulls write long letters in sand,
Dolphin leap offshore.

* * *

While reading about medieval Japanese poetry, I learned about a predecessor to our modern *haiku*, the *renga* chain of verses called *hokku* that eventually became stand-alone *haikus*. Medieval *renga* chains were often collaborative works and could be more than thirty stanzas long, but this one using nature as a metaphor for the stages of love is little more than a toe dipped in the ocean. Maybe I'll continue it at some later date, though I rather like it the way it is.

This particular *renga* began as a short poem with almost the standard syllable count for a *haiku*, close enough to count since the Japanese *on*, or sounds, in Japanese poetry don't precisely equate to our syllables even before you take translation into account. But in this early *haiku*, I left far too much of the speaker in the poem.

> *Testing the water,*
> *Dipping toes in the waves,*
> *Am I ready to swim?*

Renga – and *haiku* in general – use nature as a metaphor for something in the poet's life. When the poet speaks of himself (or herself) at all, it's in a self-effacing way that we seldom see in the West. I had a light touch of metaphor going in this *haiku*, but my focus was still too much on the person, not her natural surroundings. You may even find it obvious, upon first reading this *haiku*, that I was using thoughts about swimming in the ocean as a metaphor for thoughts about dating. That's a bit heavy-handed for any traditional Japanese style of poetry.

When I decided to join this first *haiku* to another one I'd written in order to build a *renga* off of them, I translated it stylistically into the following *haiku*. As you might imagine, the small fish could really be little fish, or they could be the speaker's toes, lined up and glistening in the water. The question the speaker asks herself in the first *haiku* is here turned into a simple statement that there is a choice waiting.

Blue water beckons,
Small fish glisten under waves,
A choice awaits.

The second stanza of this *renga* was the second of the two *haikus* that I built the rest of the *renga* on. Its location is slightly different from the first, but Japan is a land of islands and the speaker might well have her home near the ocean, like I do. The summer blooms are so numerous that the fallen ones make little summer snowdrifts – my favorite kind! – and they make the air fragrant with their perfumes. In both Oriental and Western gardens, the prevalence of the blooms places us in a feminine garden, where blooms represent women's femininity and most private anatomy (and are more appealing, at least to this woman, than are the harder lines and uninterrupted green of a masculine garden). The darkening clouds could be just the leading edge of a summer storm, but we all know that they're metaphorically more than that...

Bright blooms drift like snow,
Leaves rustle in fragrant air,
Clouds darken above.

The storm arrives, damaging the feminine flowers in the garden and sending water cascading off the roof and down the chains of bronze bells traditional Japanese houses had at the corners of their roof to keep the water somewhat together and away from the sides of the house. Rain comes down in torrents like the heavy summer storms we're very familiar with here in the South. But the storm eventually wears itself out, and life returns to the house and garden. People go back outside, even before the sun has fully emerged from behind the storm clouds.

But even with the stylistic changes to the first *hokku*, it still seemed too disconnected from the rest of the *renga*. So I added a final *hokku*, in which the speaker looks down at the ocean from her hillside home. As the storm dissipates, birds return to the shore to leave footprints that look like Japanese calligraphy, a metaphor I particularly like. Out in the depths, where the speaker was tempted to swim at the beginning of this *renga*, dolphins leap out of the water as they play. The speaker will return to the beach even if she doesn't go there today, for it is a part of her world. She may even play with the dolphins.

> *Waves below turn blue,*
> *Gulls write long letters in sand,*
> *Dolphin leap offshore.*

2

And With a Coup

The Sun's First Rays

The sun's first rays burnt off the fog, and then
His bright eyes fell upon the knight I saw approach me.
And though his face was in the dark,
I knew him by his form and stride.
I knew him well, it seemed, although
His name strayed far afield.

My heart was glad to see him; it had been too long –
And yet what was his name?
I knew if I could see his face,
My heart would shout his name in greeting.
Yet too much light behind him
Left his face in shade.

At last he had approached quite near.
'Twas here Love shot me with true aim,
For as I saw his face, I knew he was Adonis
And if my eyes deceived me not, he too was struck.
How else could one explain the look upon his face?
My heart sang out despite its mortal wound.

* * *

How many poems have been written about that magical first meeting between two lovers? For this poem, I used the same scene I would also visualize for "Before I Met Him," but focused only on the actual meeting itself.

Morning meetings have a certain amount of magic to them, as a soft sunrise turns the unknown into the familiar and the familiar into the unknown. Morning fog extends this period of mysterious familiarity. Maybe that's why the knight appears both familiar and unfamiliar until the fog of uncertainty burns away, or maybe it's because he only appears familiar in that strange way that lovers can appear familiar even at first sight.

Through most of human history, Adonis has been considered the epitome of lovers, the man all women want. In Greek mythology, he'd been the son of an unfortunate young woman, brought to Persephone to be fostered in the Underworld. But when he was grown, he was so handsome Persephone didn't want to give him back to Aphrodite. The two goddesses eventually got Zeus to make a ruling on how the young man would divide his time and attentions between them. And it somehow worked. Each woman's lover is Adonis, if only in some fragmentary way.

The medieval image of Love's arrow striking home is rather warlike and not terribly pleasant. It enters the body through the eyes, flying on until it lodges in the heart. To me, this only makes sense if the body is seen as a type of castle, with the eyes as some sort of window or aperture in the outer defenses through which a good archer could shoot to strike his target. A shot to the heart is, naturally, a mortal wound.

When First Your Eyes Met Mine

When first your eyes met mine across the way,
I could not look away despite my will.
You left, to circle round and dog my steps.
I felt your eyes upon me from behind,
Even as a hunted hind knows she's been spotted.

Many a brave hunter would wish for hounds as steady.
Glory, Chase, and Desire; yours can bring down
Any doe you'd set them after.
Guided by your huntsman Love, there is no escape.
Knowing this, I ran as for my life.

At times I thought your hounds chased other hinds,
And then I'd not be certain I would have it so.
At others, I would stop to pant and catch my breath
And suddenly your hounds would sound so close
I'd leap and run before I knew I'd heard them.

Exhausted, I found my way to a secret vale.
Your hounds then came upon me, bore me down.
Glory, Chase, Desire, and your huntsman Love,
Biting and kissing right to my very soul.
Never was hind more glad to fall.

* * *

The first version of "When First Your Eyes Met Mine" came to me late one night back when I just had a used desktop computer, so I got up and typed it up. I was certain I'd saved it, but apparently I hadn't. A power fluctuation even later that night made my computer re-boot, and I lost the poem. But my muse didn't let me off that easily, and I had to rebuild it using only the handful of lines I remembered from her visit. It didn't seem to be nearly as good as the lost poem, but there was an interesting bit of half-developed imagery in it that described courtship in hunting terms. I thought I'd go with it and see what I could do. I'm pleased with the result, though I had to rephrase the final stanza a few times to keep it from being too violent for my modern sensibilities.

When medieval nobles went hunting, they didn't go it alone. Beaters would go out and beat the bushes to drive animals toward the hunters. Huntsmen with dogs would lead the chase, and the local nobles would ride out on horseback after them. It was quite the show.

Our medieval nobles usually hunted four main types of animals. For birds like pheasants and waterfowl, falcons were the preferred method of bringing them down. The sport of falconry had been brought to England by Norman nobles in 1066 and was a form of hunting that even ladies were able to compete in. Deer were another good food source and were further differentiated between stags and does, who were also known as hinds. Stags were the more noble prey, as they sometimes attacked when they were cornered – and the graceful spread of their antlers certainly made them look really impressive. Does were an easier prey, as they were unlikely to do anything other than run and hide if they were chased. Then there were foxes, which weren't good for food but had nice warm furs and, more importantly, were canny enough to lead the hunters on a long and difficult chase. They might even get away.

Then there were the wild boars (pigs), the most dangerous and there-fore the most prestigious game animals that were commonly hunted during the Middle Ages. A wild boar, once it realized it was being hunted, would go to ground, hiding in the bushes. But if the hunters found it, it would rush out of its hiding place, attacking its attackers with its sharp tusks. It was very prestigious to be the hunter who'd taken a boar down with a spear, but more than one nobleman attempting the kill would suddenly find himself split wide open and bleeding out. The risk is what made boar the most prestigious prey animal of the time, though its delicious flesh certainly made it a welcome addition to any feast.

Obviously, the most suitable prey animal to use for this metaphor was the hind, who would run as far as she could, hide to catch her breath, and run again when she hears the hunters approaching. She has no defenses, only her speed. And since this poem uses the hunt as a metaphor for courtship instead of being a straightforward poem about hunting, she's sometimes not certain she wants to escape. By the time Love's hunting dogs bring her down, she's glad to have been caught.

I Do Not Wish

I do not wish, my love, for royal gifts from you.
No strong and towered castles with pennants flying,
No gilded mansions filled with liv'ried servants,
No chests of gold, no pearls or spice,
No fine imported silks or other worthy treasures.
For, while such gifts are rich and much to be desired,
They count as naught beside the gifts that I would have.

The gifts, my love, that I would have from you
Are rare and fine, the best that can be found.
I wish for hands that hold mine close in theirs,
For arms that hold me in embraces I would never end.
I wish for long walks and soft words with my love
And lips that give to me the very kiss of life.
These are the gifts that I wish most from you.

* * *

When reading medieval literature, one thing that stands out to the modern reader is how much the giving of showy gifts was a part of the culture. After reading the hundredth poem in which the lover gives rich gifts to his beloved, it occurred to me that someone, at some point, would want to express her own preference. As appealing as rich castles might be as gifts, is not true love a better one?

Before I Met Him

Before I met him, I had felt no love,
No deep and overwhelming passion
Poets praise and others dream of.
No handsome face enthralled me,
No timbrous voice swelled my heart.

Perhaps, as some declare, the poets lie,
Painting treacherous lust with fairer form and name.
Perhaps I was unworthy, incapable of love,
Or even – God forbid – one who could not love a man.
It must be one of these, I knew.

Yet I was wrong, this I learned when first we met.
Love had sent Adonis to me, Apollo had delivered him.
I told myself this was not true –
My heart knew better even then.
I swore I was a fool to think it might be so.

Who could not love him? This man is formed
With true perfection in each limb and sinew, heart and soul.
He moves with equal ease at tourney and in dance.
His eyes deep pools in which I always fall
His hands guide me in the dance and feel so right in mine.

I would be his forever, each moment and each hour.
Give myself to him in orchard and in chamber.
Slip away to lie amid the roses or the reeds,
Spend long summer days under the silk of his pavilion,
And longer winter nights on the floor by his fire.

Yet I must keep my distance, if indeed I can.
Each tender touch of hand becomes a long caress.
Each simple kiss is followed by ten more.
Fate drives me toward him without ceasing.
Others will see the change in me, and talk.

* * *

Courtly love poetry varied greatly from its start in twelfth century France until its evolution into later forms of love poetry, especially since it was written in the language of the people – the local dialect of Provençal, French, Italian, English, and even German – instead of the educated Latin of the time. Most of these works were written by men, but a few gave voice to the female experience of the time. Their poems combined a naïve voice with an overtly frank sexuality that I found refreshingly intimate.

The young lady in this poem doesn't really expect to ever find love, believing that it will surely pass her by if it even exists. Then one morning, Love surprises her with a lover who is the very embodiment of the high-medieval knightly ideal. More than that, her lover is so handsome that she considers him an Adonis, like the mortal man who became Aphrodite's lover (as well as Persephone's, but that's another story).

I borrowed the places where the lady wants to be alone with her Adonis from several of the medieval poems that inspired me, which you'll have to read for yourself. These sources also explain the need for secrecy, because a medieval love affair brought with it some very real dangers.

3

The Other Side

When He is With Me

When he is with me, joy is unbound.
My lips burn with the passion of his kisses.
My skin tingles with the intensity of his touch.
My soul finds wings in his embrace.

When we are apart, joy turns to torment.
My lips ache with need for one small kiss.
My skin is cold, far from the heat of his fire.
My soul would trade Paradise to be in his arms.

* * *

This is the first of my poems that were inspired by the more angsty of the medieval courtly love poems I'd read – yes, the angst we now associate with teenagers goes back to at least the Middle Ages, and there's a whole subtype of medieval love poems that read like they were written by the medieval version of angsty teenagers.

The lovers' passion is intense, something everyone would dream of sharing with someone special. But when the lady's lover is away, his absence becomes a torment.

When He Does Not Look at Me

When he does not look at me,
My heart quakes with fear that he no longer loves me.
Yet one glance brings relief,
For I cannot miss the love that dwells in his eyes.
How can I bear his absence,
When I have only my fears for company?

* * *

With this poem, we continue with the theme of the torment of absence, or at least the torment of the lack of contact. The lady's fears are relieved whenever she sees the love in his eyes, but she seems to have such a short memory whenever he goes away.

Why do I do This?

Why do I do this?
What sort of fool am I
To think that your great ocean
Would ever be satisfied
To touch my sandy beaches
Without ripping all my sand away,
Without returning far too soon –
As if for the first time –
And demanding to know
Why I hide
All my sand
From you?

* * *

There might not be quite as many poems about the end of love as there are about its heady early days, but the misused or forgotten lover is a common poetic trope, even – or especially – during the heyday of the fashion for courtly love poetry. We've all been there, unfortunately, even our ancestresses in bliauts (a beautiful fashionable dress from the twelfth century).

Oddly enough, even though I was reading copious courtly love poems when I wrote this poem, the structure is modern and the imagery is clearly based on one of my favorite aspects of life here in Florida. It marries well with the poignancy expressed in these regretful courtly love poems.

You Must Know

You must know that I do not
Long for the sweetness of your embrace,
Or wish that you would kiss my lips again.
For I am not another wistful maiden,
Longing always for the one who left.
You think me a fool if you think me such.
I only wish you were but half the man
I thought you were.
If indeed you were that man,
I would be with you always.

* * *

And then there's the lover who, far from being an abuser with boundary issues, is simply so much less than what he'd first appeared to be that his lover can only wish he'd lived up to a fraction of the man he'd first passed himself off as. And yet, it seemeth to me that the lady doth protest just a little too much to be fully believed. If the lover is a fool, we all have a touch of the fool in us at times.

Prince of my Heart

Prince of my heart,
The way I feel toward you
Makes me wish I trusted
In the good will of Venus.

* * *

That fool gives us the hope we need to try again with someone else, even if we're a little less trusting this time. Surely Venus wants to see some of her worshippers in happy relationships, non?

4

Love and War

Since First our Peoples Met

Since first our peoples met in ages past,
Most neighborly we've been.
We've greeted each new king of yours
With gifts of royal bounty.

We sent you wagonloads of food
Whene'er your lands were bare
And sent you everything we could
Whene'er you were in need.

But you mistook our graciousness
For weakness, I now see.
Our virtues made you think that we
Were ripe for plunderer's waste.

Your doom rides hard upon you
For our men know well their craft.
Their swords are sharp, their skill is true,
Their steeds are fast and strong.

The foe has never yet been born
Who'll stand against our men,
Nor wrest us from our homes and lands,
Nor see us kneel before a conquering foe.

For if by some ill-fated chance
You should win past our men,
'Tis only that your fate it is
To die by female hands.

* * *

This is one of my favorite poems, even though it's less directly about love than several of my more beautiful poems. What can I say? I like the speaker's spunk, her pride, and her love of her people.

The giving of gifts was a major part of ancient and medieval cultures, in Europe and around the world. But gift-giving was supposed to be – or at least seem to be – either an equal exchange of goods or a payment for services rendered. Northern lords like Beowulf were known as "ring-givers" for the arm-rings and other jewelry they gave their men, and fealty was a formal exchange where a king gave land in exchange for an oath of loyalty that included the number of men the new lord would bring to his king's army whenever it was called up. Kings visiting each other or sending ambassadors to each other's courts would give rich gifts in exchange for the goods they expected to receive, even engaging in a certain amount of one-upmanship.

The speaker and her people have always been good gift-givers toward their neighbors, but their gifts are never reciprocated. Worse, the other kingdom seems to be rather unstable, running through kings fast enough that there might be civil wars or assassinations involved. Possibly due to this instability, they experience periods of famine when their survival depends on outright charity from the speaker's kingdom. These gifts go unappreciated, but invading the speaker's kingdom might be their last mistake.

The speaker is justly proud of her kingdom's knights, but the fighting ability of her kingdom's women also has historical precedent. The Middle Ages were an era when even lesser lords had their own armies and needed them, both for their own battles and so they would be ready when the king summoned the armies. Even among the common-ers, women needed to be able to defend their homes and lands while their men were away. Noblewomen had to be prepared to command armies and defend their castles, either because the men were away or because the men who were around wanted to take their patrimony or that of their child. Noblewomen might even act as aggressors or lead their own armies on crusade.

Eleanor of Aquitaine, who became queen of both France and Eng-land in turn, was probably a bit more of a firecracker than most women. When she went on crusade with her first husband, she brought along more knights than he did, a situation that couldn't have pleased him unless Louis was so goal-oriented that he cared more about the total number of knights than he cared about who brought them. She later "raised Poitou" (one of the territories she brought to her marriages, full of knights who were in fealty to her) and took part in their sons' re-bellion against her second husband, supported her eldest surviving son Richard against his younger brother once Richard became king, and finally supported her youngest son John against her grandson Arthur's bid for the throne. Over significant stretches of her 82 years, the course of major historical events depended on whether she controlled large enough armies and sufficiently stout castles.

Eleanor seems to have made a habit of taking things up a notch, but many other women had to defend their family's lands while their husbands were away or after they were left widowed with a minor child as heir to the estate(s). Several other queens and ladies – always better known to history than average women – also defended the home front at significant times and were said to have had "the heart of a man." Le Cid's widow, Donna Jimena, defended and held Valencia for more than a year from 1001 to 1002, organizing her army to "beat off Muslim attacks." Blanche of Castile, widow of King Louis VIII of France, had to suppress the many rebellious vassals who saw young Louis IX's minor-ity as an opportunity to take more power for themselves, taking her armies into the field to tame them and stop an English invasion that was supported by her son's rebellious vassals in Brittany. After losing both her first husband, King Richard Coeur-de-Lion, and her second husband, Count Thibaut III de Champagne, Blanche de Navarre made substantial use of both warfare and diplomacy to protect her son and his patrimony of Champagne.

Christine de Pizan, the first professional female writer in Europe, strongly recommended military training for noble daughters because of the numerous situations that could make it necessary for women to go to war. In 1405, she wrote in *Le Trésor de la Citie des Dames* (*The Treasure of the City of Ladies*) that the wife of a nobleman should:

> ...have the heart of a man... know how to use weapons and be familiar with everything that pertains to them, so that she may be ready to command her men if the need arises... know how to launch an attack or defend against one [and]... take care that her fortresses are well garrisoned.

The idea of women defending the castle was so commonplace that it led to a popular literary metaphor, the allegorical siege of the Castle of Love, which was portrayed in art and literature and acted out in early plays. The earliest artistic depictions I've found of this siege date from the early fourteenth century, about a hundred years after the earliest records of it being acted out. Ladies, usually armed with roses and other similar armaments, would defend the castle against an attacking force of men trying to storm the castle with similar weaponry. If the men succeeded in taking the castle, they won the love of the women who'd defended it – which they're reported to have done in almost every one of these allegorical plays except for those performed in Queen Elizabeth I's court (go figure!). Early in Henry VIII's courtship of Elizabeth's mom Anne Boleyn, she was cast as Lady Perseverance in a Castle of Love play where Henry was part of the besieging force. I might need to write a poem about one of these plays at some point, though maybe not the one that helped Henry win Anne's hand and thereby ultimately helped lead to her death.

So there was a long tradition of women at least leading and possibly forming the defending forces in any medieval last line of defense, and the speaker in "Since First our Peoples Met" knows she has good reason to be certain of how well even the women of her people will defend themselves and their kingdom. The invading army is dead already, they just don't know it yet.

A friend of mine, when I lived close enough to her to attend the same poetry circles, would always exclaim "hooah!" right after I finished each recitation of this poem.

She gets it.

I Gave you my Chemise

I gave you my chemise before you left,
Took you to our chamber and slipped it on
Under all your clothes, after we had
Held each other privily once more.

I put my chemise on you before you left,
The silk stretched tight across your chest
Though loose on mine, and all I wished
Was that you could return it to me soon.

I watched from my window as you
Rode off with all your men for Outremer.
I watched and wept, with fear so deep
That you might never ride this way again.

I pray each day for you, my lord.
I pray to notre Dame, that yours not feel her loss.
I pray to the Magdalene, that I not mourn for you.
I pray to the Jhesu, that you not make his sacrifice.

And though the priest might burn me for it,
I pray to my mother's gods.
For any who might save you are mine,
And I care only that they bring you home again.

* * *

Years ago, I read a short little history about a German woman named Una. She gave her husband her chemise right off her body and dressed him in it before he left on crusade, asking him to not take it off until he took it off to return it to her. He wore it under his own clothes and armor, then seems to have been able to give it back when he was done.

I loved the romance of the idea, even though anything worn for so long in the heat of the crusader territories would be fit only to be burned afterwards! There also seemed to be an undercurrent of magic to the gift, which inspired me to add the last verse, with its reference to the layers of belief systems that were present in medieval life.

My Love Rides off to War

My love rides off to war
Companioned by the full contingent
Of his men, and yet he is alone
For I ride not with him.

The enemy he goes to fight
Have set the very ground afire with hate.
They must be devils, I am sure
For no man can live in such a hell.

" 'Tis no right place for woman fair," said he,
"The very beasts and winds would drive us out."
'Tis no right place for men so true,
But he sees duty, and obliges.

They'd drive all evil out and bring
A new peace to places holy.
But can they keep this evil out
When it would have dominion?

I would be brave and strong for him,
Believe he will return in peace and glory.
But can it be that men alive
Can fight – and win – against this deadly foe?

* * *

My protagonist here is a lady whose lover is leaving her to win fame and glory – not to mention eternal salvation – serving on crusade. In my personal interpretation, the war he is off to serve in is the Third Crusade, possibly the most famous of the crusades and the last one to achieve any kind of real success. It was called the crusade of three kings, though one of the crusader kings died before he even reached the Holy Land and the other two were more competitors than allies. At least in the literature, Richard I "Cœur-de-Lion" of England and the Saracen sultan and general Salah al-Din "Saladin" respected each other as honorable enemies more than either of them respected Philippe II "Philippe Auguste" of France.

This respect, if it wasn't an invention of the bards and court historians, was quite unusual both for its time and for all time. Whether the enemy attack was unprovoked and horrific or the causes of the war are more difficult to ascertain, we tend to dehumanize our enemies and speak of them in ways that make it seem necessary to kill them even if it isn't. The invading English, during the Hundred Years' War, became "les goddams" because their use of that curse goes back at least that far and because it's probably the most suitable thing to say when you see a gang of them riding for your farm on *chevauchée* (a military raid on civilians, because the Geneva Conventions hadn't been invented yet). During more recent wars, the Germans became "the huns," "les boches," and "krauts." In today's wars, we have "infidels" and "nazis," with as little care for proof as the English needed for "huns" and less than the French and Americans needed for their cabbage-based terms.

But the warrior on the ground is almost always fighting on behalf of his (or possibly, even back in the Middle Ages, her) family and loved ones, regardless of his leaders' reason for the war. Those who love him care more for his safe return than for why he went to war in the first place. Now and throughout history, the loved ones who stay behind wish only for their warrior' safe return.

My True King

My true king, you call yourself
Barbaric, uncouth, an old man
Bent and broken before his time.

My love, you still remain to me
The strong young prince you were
Before your battles scarred you.

Your victories won, your lands defended,
Let the warmth of my fire restore to you
All that you think is lost.

* * *

With war, even those knights who return home don't really come back in one piece. Those who return home both need and deserve to love and be loved by someone who sees beyond the scars. It's time to come home and be healed, at least emotionally.

The lady's lover is a true exemplar of the ideal nobleman of the era, a king and knight who won the battles he faced in defending his people and lands. For that matter, this type of man is one we still need today, the soldier and first responder who risks his life every day for his people. This man has done his duty, putting himself between his people and their enemies for many years, and now his body pays the price.

The lady loves him even though he no longer looks like the handsome young prince he once was, perhaps in part because of how he got his battle scars. The fire she offers to warm him with could be simply literal, but in this type of poem we can generally expect a hidden meaning as well. In this double entendre, she offers him a warm seat by the fire while also telling him that she wishes to re-awaken the passion he believes is behind him.

Pucelle

Girl from the countryside, pucelle.
Known to nobody, a nothing.
How can you think that God above
Would send His saints to sign you to His cause?

Girl from the countryside, pucelle.
A little thing, a plain bird.
How can you think our rightful king
Would listen to you if to court you came?

Girl from the countryside, pucelle.
A girl in boy's clothes, armed with a pretty sword.
How can you think our noble generals
Would listen to a child playing dress-up?

Girl from the countryside, pucelle.
Savior of Orleans, of France itself.
How could you think your victories
Would get our young king crowned?

Girl from the countryside, pucelle.
Victor imprisoned, victorious no more.
How can you think our gracious king
Would save you now he wears the golden crown?

Girl from the countryside, pucelle.
Brave child questioned by Church lawyers.
How can you out-think them like you do
Yet not be the witch they say you are?

Girl from the countryside, pucelle.
A white-clad victim on a burning stake.
How can you know Our Lord above
Will take you up to Heaven when you call His name?

Girl from the countryside, pucelle.
Our champion when all hope has died.
Watch from above and bless our land
That you gave everything you had to save.

* * *

A *pucelle*, literally speaking, is a female flea (*puce*). And yes, that's where we got the name of that weird color between purple and brown. *Pucelle* is thought to have Latin roots that make it mean "virgin," though it was also a term used by the aristocracy to talk about peasant girls. That's presumably how the word picked up its risqué meaning.

Okay, so that part of my family tree wasn't exactly nice to the peasantry, but the French nobility weren't uncommon in that respect.

They were uncommon in that they gave new significance to the term when they were writing or talking about Jehanne d'Arc, whom you anglophones know as Joan of Arc. They made the term *Pucelle* into a term of honor, a familiar nickname for your favorite saint. If your only exposure to the term were biographies of Joan, you wouldn't know about the flea connection, let alone the salacious stuff – unless maybe you were reading an iconoclastic biography that tries to explain away some of the more supernatural parts of her story by saying she imagined them because she had psychological issues due to [insert their favorite salacious theory]. And their theory du jour might even make sense, at least until you think about the fact that few people, even without psychological issues, are anywhere near as successful as this simple peasant girl was.

Jehanne d'Arc has been my favorite saint since sometime early in elementary school, and we're not even Catholic. I remember devouring everything I could find about her and wishing I could dress like her, even as a little child. She's almost certainly one of the earliest and most significant reasons for my fascination with medieval France, especially since my family is from the same part of France as she was. She could be a distant cousin. Or aunt.

Jehanne was born around 1412 in Domrémy, a village just barely on the French side of the border with the Holy Roman Empire (modern Germany) and nominally considered to be part of Burgundian territory (the part of France ruled by a line of turncoat dukes who sided with England instead of France). When she was born, the two kingdoms were almost halfway through the Hundred Years' War, that period when the French Crown's most troublesome vassal, the kings of England, decided that the French lands they held as vassals of the French Crown and the fact that they'd occasionally married French princesses meant that they had the right to claim the French throne. Not surprisingly, the French Crown, nobles, and people took exception to that claim – pretty much everyone but the dukes of Burgundy and their closest followers. French losses were tragic, and the English took their terrible *chevauchées* across the French countryside and into towns and villages like Domrémy.

At 13, Jehanne started to see visions, who eased her fears and told her that they were St. Michael the Archangel and two female saints, Catherine and Margaret. They had been sent from God to tell her of her vital mission to save France by expelling the nation's enemies and getting its rightful king, the Dauphin Charles, crowned king. Whether she was aware of it or not in her distant part of France, there was a popular prophecy that a virgin would come to save the kingdom, which had been lost by a queen (presumably the French queen Isabeau de Bavarie, who had been forced to sign the Treaty of Troyes, thereby disinheriting the French Dauphin Charles and making the English king heir to the French throne).

France's fortunes had ebbed almost as far as they possibly could. Only something truly impressive could save France, and that something was Jehanne.

It took determination for this teenage girl to get from Domrémy to Chinon, where the French royal court was in residence. Even once she arrived, most people at court thought of her as something of a curiosity, an amusing topic of conversation but nothing significant. To be taken seriously, she had to pick the Dauphin out of a crowd and tell him something that startled him, something that's still a mystery. Then she had to go through a medical examination to prove she was a virgin – because God wouldn't use an 'unclean' vessel – and be interrogated by theological leaders associated with the royal court. Only then, after about a month, did she finally get the Dauphin's permission and support for her mission, which freed the city of Orléans within nine days of her arrival on that front. Within two months, her armies had gone on to free Beaugency, Sully-sur-Loire, Troyes, Châlons, and the cathedral city of Reims.

Reims, of course, was a vital win. Medieval French kings were crowned in multiple cathedrals across the royal domain, but Reims was special, the first place any king was crowned and the place where his coronation made him truly the king of France. Without a coronation in Reims, Charles was nothing more than the French dauphin. With that coronation, he was truly the king of France.

When I read a biography of Jehanne in the sixth grade, I remember thinking Charles should marry Jehanne and have her crowned queen beside him. He owed his throne to this beautiful and powerful young woman, what could be more natural than for him to put her beside him on it?

Of course, if you know anything about medieval culture, you know why that could never have happened. Jehanne was a peasant, not a princess. She was a curiosity and barely acceptable as a tool; the kind of weapon you might be embarrassed to need and not feel any particular loyalty toward once she stops being useful. It's worth noting that the men and generals who served under her were loyal to her even though the Crown and court often were not, because they saw her miraculous successes firsthand. But Charles turned his back on Jehanne after her leadership and faith got him crowned. Instead, he started paying more attention to courtiers who believed she was becoming too powerful and needed to be put in her place. Within a year, she had been abandoned by her king and captured by the Burgundians. A year later, she had been murdered by the English.

The first known professional female author, Christine de Pizan, had retired to a convent (probably the Dominican convent of Poissy) in 1415 after the tragic French losses at Azincourt (Agincourt). For almost fifteen years, she didn't write anything as far as we know – a painfully-long dry spell for a writer that speaks to a complete change of direction and great disappointment in her life.

But then she heard about Jehanne's early victories and Charles' coronation. Bursting with excitement and new-found optimism, Christine wrote her last surviving work, the sixty-one stanza *Ditié de Jehanne d'Arc*. The *Ditié* is nothing more nor less than an outburst of joyful song on paper. The wave of joy and optimism that swept France alongside news of Jehanne's repeated successes leaps off the page in a way we seldom see in historical works. I've quoted one of these stanzas, to give you a taste of the importance of Jehanne's victories to the people of France. It seemed obvious to Christine that God had sent Jehanne, greatest of heroes, to save France from the English, elevate Charles to the throne of France, and lead him to retake the Holy Land and become emperor of all nations. If she had truly received the support of Charles VII and his court, perhaps Jehanne could have accomplished even the last and most difficult of the three impossible deeds Christine believed God had sent Jehanne to accomplish.

Song of Joan
Stanza XII

And you, Charles, king of the French
Seventh of your high name,
Who in such a great war have long been
Unable to take much success:
But, thanks to God, we see your renown
High elevated by the Maid,
Who made to submit under your banner
Your enemies (such a new thing!)

Christine de Pisan, 1429

Aude's Song

1   *The most beauteous maid in all the realm*
They once did call me with the pride of kin.
My mother claimed God meant me for a prince.
I knew not then what grief their love would bring
As I grew, sheltered by my kith and kin
In lands where peace was past.

2   *The Emperor made war 'gainst mine uncle*
Girart, the one who in his youth was tricked
By Charles' wily queen so that he gave
The kiss of homage on her foot instead
Of on the king's, and I knew naught of this,
The font of all my grief.

3   *T'was many years Emperor Charles besieged*
Mine Uncle Girart's city of Vienne.
Seven years our men the French impassèd,
They'd fight our men but never win an ell.
The French decided then that they would host
A tournament before our city walls.
My grief was born that day.

4 *I was a woman grown by then, a maid*
Of ten-and-seven years and graceful mien.
On that fine day, I'd loosened up my cloak
To let it spread behind me as a train
And show the silken shoulders of my gown.
I'd only thought to represent my kin
With all the grace and beauty God allowed
If I had known the future then, would I
Elude both love and grief?

5 *Rollant rode at my brother, all prepared*
To joust with him and learn for once and all
Which one the greater warrior was, the best
In all the lands of France or its marchès.
But then he saw me, turned and swiftly rode
To catch me by the waist and lift me up
Behind him and astride his destrier.
He would have ridden back behind French lines
To do with me according to his will,
But that my dear Oliviers chased him down.
I heard him promise Duke Rollant my hand
In marriage noble if he would but wait.
A joust, he said, would be the heavy price
Rollant must pay if he would have my hand.
Grief took firm aim that day.

6 *King Charles' men besieged Vienne itself,*
His armies then arrayed in force against
Our city walls – I ventured forth upon
The high stone wall that on the meadow side
Surrounded our fair town and kept it safe
The knights of France looked distant, small, until
They propped their ladders up against our walls
And clambered up them, weapons in their hands.

My ladies screamed when they first saw Gascons
Swarm up a ladder closer than our stair.
We were not armed, but stones lay close around.
I grabbed the largest one near me and dropped
It on the closest Gascon soldier there.
His helmet broke, a piece flew off and he
Fell, bloody, hit the man who followed next
So both and seven others fell to ground
I hoped they'd breathe no more.

7   But Rollant saw the Gascons fall, and he
Rode laughing to the broken ladder base.
He leapt onto the ramparts, landed there
Six ells away from where my ladies wailed.
He praised my prowess, swore they would not take
This point upon the wall where ladies fought
But he would know my name if I feared not
To name myself, my people, and my kin.
I answered boldly, naming all of them.
And then he turned away as if in grief.
I knew a knight so brave must have a love
Whose beauty was beyond compare but not
That in his eyes I was that nonpareil.
Nor that he thought Oliviers was bound
To kill him or be killed by him and thus
To terminate our love.

8   The morn that followed, Oliviers rode out
To cross the Rhône from Vienne to that isle
Where first he'd challenged Rollant o'er a bird.
They fought a battle dreadful as can be.
No mortal knights could ever beat Rollant,
None yet could challenge Oliviers and live.
They slashed and parried, slashed and hacked away.

Each blow broke gems from helms and rings from mail,
Till all who watched were certain both would die.
A pause – had one succumbed? But then they'd fight
As if they could not tire but were locked in
Combat eternal with the foe each loved
As brothers do. Would my grief be so great
If Rollant that day had died, when I had
Just begun to love him?

9   I prayed each moment of the day that they
     Might both survive, that by some miracle there
     Might grow a peace between these men I love.
     T'was even when a fog rose up and hid
     The land so thick we could not see a thing.
     But then a blaze erupted from that isle
     So bright the shadows it cast in the hall
     Were clear as at noonday. We knew not what
     To think was happening below or if
     Our knights could live. It dissipated then;
     They both emerged and Oliviers told us
     Of marriage arranged between Rollant's
     Fair cousin Ermengarde and Oliviers,
     And one arranged 'tween Rollant and myself.
     I thanked God for the miracle that seemed
     To save the men I love the most, but Grief
     Must surely have his way.

10   Some few days later, Ermengarde arrived,
     Her mother, aunt, and kindred all in train.
     She swore her troth at matins then beside
     Oliviers as we swore our troth as well.
     She wed him that next even with a feast
     Where Rollant charmed me with his grace at dance
     As much as his prowess in battle had.

He made me promises of how our feast
And wedding night would pass. But all my grief
Grew in that moment, though I knew it not.
His promises were fog.

11   My mother and the women of the court
All brought for me great chests of bright and gold-
Embroidered gowns for me to don as bride
Of great king Charles' greatest knight. The feast
To celebrate our nuptials was being
Baked and spitted in the kitchens, the wines
Had been brought up and mixed for all to share.
The preparations all were made, and we
Would have our wedding feast that night. My grief
Seemed just a distant thing.

12   But dreams of vespers died at none when
Sore envoys reached the court and told our king
Of Gascoigne invaded, Tarragonne
Razed, of Bordeaux besieged, of Orléans,
Of Bourges and all of France in gravest need.
All in gravest danger if th'Emperor
Failed to defend the people of his realm
With all his armies, brought in greatest haste.
Great Charlemagne swore to God above
He needed now the wisest service of
His lords to crush the breed who threatened those
Who looked to him for their defense on earth,
The duty of a king.

13   Archbishop Arno then declared that all
Who fought alongside th'Emperor would find
Their sins washed clean in Heaven's lofty rolls
Great Charlemagne to his barons gave

Leave to go home and raise their armies, then
Meet him and all his men in far Narbonne
Where they would meet in battle all who sought
To occupy our lands. My father then
With uncles three, great Charles gave defense
Of all our eastern marches and the south.
My heart grew cold, when first I saw unfurled
Grief's banners first advance.

14   *My love came to me while the forces of*
The French prepared to ride in Charles' great train.
His thoughts were on the war, I knew although
He greeted me with passion in his eyes
And on his lips a kiss that stole my breath.
He swore he would return, would marry me
Before compline the day that he returned,
That he would stay and wed me now except
That enemies are best fought far from home,
Before the danger reaches those he loves.
He said he'd not allow them closer than
They were to me that day. I lost him then,
Although I knew it not.

15   *Seven long years they battled in the Spains,*
Seven long years while Queen Bertrande ruled
In France and my sweet sister Ermengarde
Raised up the fine young son of Oliviers.
Those years I waited, on my knees I prayed
For what God could not give.

16   *Messengers came to us at harvest time,*
Brought news of knights deceivèd and a great
Battle fought when vict'ry appeared complete.
My grief attacked, spoke words the messengers
Would choose to never say.

17   *All watched days later as the Emperor*
Led his armies into Aix city.
I spoke to him while soldiers still rode in.
My grief spurred on ahead to claim the prize.
"Fair child," great Charles said, tears in his beard,
"France suffers now losses beyond measure,
And you have lost more than the rest of us.
For we have lost the kingdom's greatest knights –
Your love Rollant, your brother Oliviers,
Ten thousand more among our noblest knights."
My grief broke down my gates.

18   *King Charles took my hands in his. Quoth he,*
"Fair daughter, I know well that you must weep,
But when spring comes again, I wish to wed
You to Prince Louis, he who is my heir."
Grief burned my towns and sowed my fields in salt.
I could not speak, for though at heart I knew
Prince Louis was as great as my Rollant
And to wed him would bring me much honor,
I could not speak to tell our great king Charles
No man could match Duke Rollant in my eyes.
My world had died with him.

19   *I fell into a swoon; I knew no more.*
A knight of Queen Bertrande's carried me
Up to her chamber, where they hoped I'd wake.
Six long days passed, naught could restore my life.

My heart had stopped with news of my great loss.
The seventh day, they said my soul had passed.
A great procession then great Charles made
Four countesses he sent to bring me home
To Saint Denis, the royal convent there,
Where I would be entombed.

20   *I woke in chapel where six novices*
Prepared my body for eternal rest,
The countesses then told me all that passed.
They thought to bring me home to court a queen,
But I shall serve my God right here until
He reunites me with my love upon
The day that brings me joy.

* * *

One subject I've long wanted to write a poem about is Aude, the barely-mentioned maiden in the *Chanson de Roland* (*Song of Roland*) who's the sister of the French nobleman Oliviers (Oliver) and the fiancée of Rolant (Roland), the eponymous hero of the work and the nephew of the Emperor Charlemagne.

Did I mention that Aude is barely mentioned in the *Chanson de Roland*?

In the entire four-thousand-line work, she's mentioned in twenty-nine of two hundred ninety-one stanzas. Most of that is toward the end of the work, where Charlemagne tells her that Roland is dead and offers her his son Loewis (Louis, as we would spell his name today) as a replacement fiancé. The news kills her, so Charlemagne sends a funeral cortege of four countesses and various other attendants to take her body to a royal convent for burial. That's about as much as you can expect any *chanson de geste* (song/poem of great deeds) to delve into the hero's romantic interest. She exists, she dies of grief when he dies. Wow.

We can't even be sure that she inspired some of his great deeds (the purpose of ladies in these works), because Roland isn't all that expressive as a lover. Her brother Oliver talks about her more than Roland does, and that's not much.

For a work as influential as the *Chanson de Roland*, it seemed impossible that nobody had ever expanded on her story. Was she really that uninteresting to the medieval authors who were so moved by *Roland* and the other great epic cycles?

With a bit of research, I found an end to my frustration. In the 12th century, Bertrand de Bar-Sur-Aube had written the *Chanson de Girart de Vienne* (the *Song of Girart of Vienna*). This is one of the great French cycles, a long poem that tells the story of the rise to power and prominence of Aude's father and uncles, four brothers whose noble father's lands had been ravaged by the deprecations of King Sinagon and his followers in one of the Moorish invasions of southern Europe in the early 8th century. The four young men set out to make their fortunes and are all successful, though Girart – like the historical Count Gerardus of Vienne, on whom he was based – finds himself besieged by Charlemagne for insisting that his county was an *allod* (inherited property, in this case from his wife's father) instead of a *fief* he only held at the pleasure of his king. This made him a legendary symbol of the wronged but honorable nobleman, who only rebelled because his rights were being trampled by the king to whom he'd sworn his loyalty and to whom he was still loyal.

The *Chanson de Girart* and other accounts of Gerardus were popular from the western end of Provence to northern Burgundy and probably beyond, due to regional pride and the area's tradition of being a touch antiroyalist. And maybe this antiroyalist tradition explains certain decisions made later, durng the Hundred Years War.

Aude and Roland meet in the *Chanson de Girart* and are engaged by the end of the poem, as part of the peace process. After things fall apart between Charlemagne and his proud but honorable vassal Marquis Girart, Charlemagne and his forces chase Girart out of France and into the eastern marches where Vienne is. ["Marquis" was an equivalent title to "count" during the Middle Ages and was used for the lords of lands in the wild marches on the edge of a kingdom, though Girart is also called a "duke" in the *Chanson*.] Charlemagne sends for reinforcements, especially his young nephew Roland "of bright and fair complexion" (line 2519), who has already earned a reputation for bravery (line 2669). Young Aude and her brother Oliver come with their father Renier when he brings his armies to Vienne to reinforce Girart's. Roland and Oliver soon meet and argue over a hunting falcon. Oliver is quickly knighted and earns a reputation that matches Roland's, but it isn't until seven years later that Roland plans a joust outside the city in hopes of drawing out Girart's forces. Here, he meets Aude, who – like all the other ladies of the castle – comes out to watch the fighting. Roland turns from his fight with Oliver – the main reason he had planned this joust – and captures Aude, intending to bring her back to the French camp and have his way with her. Oliver challenges Roland to a fight while he's on his way back to the French lines with Aude and is able to save her.

Several other encounters between Roland and one or both of the siblings follow, culminating in an all-day duel between our two heroes that ends when an angel descends in answer to Aude's prayer and tells them to make peace and save their strength for fighting the Saracens who have conquered the Iberian Peninsula and are now crossing the Pyrenees into France. Part of the peace process is the decision that Aude will marry Roland, though they first have to get peace declared between Charlemagne and Girart so they can make the engagement official. But just when it looks like they are about to celebrate a wedding, messengers from Gascony arrive with news of the invasion that the angel had warned Roland and Oliver about. The Saracens have invaded Gascony and are about to take Bordeaux. The wedding is postponed and, if you've ever read the *Chanson de Roland*, you know why it was tragically never consummated.

I could do a lot with this! Aude is hardly a powerless Victorian lady, though like them she's beautiful enough to make even our heroic Roland completely forget what he is doing. This bold maiden castigates

Roland for his part in the war between Charlemagne and her uncle, and on one occasion she impresses Roland by casually dropping a stone from the top of Vienne's walls onto the head of an attacking Gascon, nearly killing the man (yes, I made her great deed more impressive in the poem). Roland is the epitome of a medieval man's man, so this appeals to him in the same way that a pretty girl at a gun range who shoots well is even more attractive to the men there than a pretty girl who can't. And Aude definitely appreciates Roland's attention, because he's as much her ideal man as she's his ideal woman.

But I also needed to make some changes. I couldn't give our greatest knight and our fairest maiden a wedding without going against the literary canon, but nobody mentioned Oliver's romantic life. And since women's chances of dying in childbirth back then were approximately the same as men's likelihood of dying in battle, it wouldn't be uncommon for more than one peace-weaving marriage to be made in hopes of bringing warring families together, a process anthropologists and historians call "reciprocal female exogamy" when the marriages are basically a bride swap. Thus, we have Roland's fair cousin Ermengarde, who at least gets to be properly married before she's widowed. She gets to raise the son she created with her husband, something Aude must have envied her for as she waited for Roland to return.

To make Aude able to speak for herself in this poem the way I wanted to, I also had to change her death at the end of *Roland* to something else. The news of her losses could plausibly make her catatonic, but she would eventually wake from that. Especially if she had already been taken to the convent by then, it would be in character for her to decide to stay there until God reunites her with Roland. There are even lines in *Girart* that can be taken as foreshadowing that she would end up in a convent if Roland died.

I composed the *Chanson d'Aude* in the same format as the *Chanson de Roland* and the *Chanson de Girart*, just a lot shorter – twenty stanzas instead of two hundred ninety-one or one hundred and ninety-two respectively. Audiences have changed, and I'm not sure anyone would ever read my song for Aude if it were a full-length book unless it were in prose.

The stanzas (also known as *laisses*) are more like paragraphs than the stanzas we're more familiar with are. They're composed of as many lines as they need for whatever happens in them, like paragraphs. Each line, however, is ten syllables long and written in iambic pentameter, with a *caesura* (a pause often signified with a comma), usually located just after the fourth or sixth syllable. A six-syllable unrhymed line called a *vers orphelin* (orphan verse) terminates each stanza and often gives the impression that it acts as a kind of "tl:dr" ("too long: didn't read," in case anyone's not up on internet slang) summary of the stanza's major point.

This format of long lines followed by one short line is both easier and harder than our usual poetic forms. You would think having an un-limited number of lines available for each stanza would make it almost as easy to write as a prose paragraph is, but the total number of syllables in each "paragraph" always has to equal $10x + 6$, where $x =$ the number of lines in the stanza. In addition, the whole poem needs to be written in iambic pentameter, a pattern of stressed and unstressed syllables most of us only know about because William Shakespeare used it heavily.

This poetic meter has been in use since at least the twelfth century and seems to be related to the hexameters used in Classical Greek and Roman poetry. And it's no surprise that poetry using five or six iambs per line has been with us all this time, because the pattern of unstressed and stressed syllables creates a "bu-BUM bu-BUM bu-BUM" rhythm that echoes the beat of the human heart. If that's not a rhythm designed to help speakers and their audiences remember a poem, I don't know what is.

I'd like to add two final notes, for readers who are unfamiliar with medieval culture.

People in Aude's era used different ways to measure distances than we use now. The long unit of measure (like the meter or yard) of the Middle Ages was the *ell*, though its exact length varied depending on the region. Since these lengths ranged from approximately 0.69 meters/ 27 inches up to 1.14 meters/45 inches, we can roughly translate an *ell* to a meter or yard. Roland was only about six meters or yards away from Aude and her ladies when he leapt up onto the battlements of Vienne for their encounter on the wall.

Time was another part of life that was measured differently. Medieval people were less focused on the clock than we are and generally used the canonical hours of the local church, because it was easy to tell when the monks or nuns were celebrating the different hours of the daily liturgy. *Matins* took place between midnight and dawn. *None* was the mid-afternoon service, around 3pm. *Vespers* was the evening service, while *compline* ended the day and prepared the soul for sleep and death. *Even* wasn't one of these canonical hours but was a shortened form of "evening" – approximately vespers, then. So the dreams Aude wakes with, of a wedding day and a bright future with her love, die at mid-afternoon, when their wedding preparations are almost complete. That must have made her loss even more painful!

5

True Loves

Although She Does
Not Know

Although she does not know it yet
She is the lodestone to my very life.
Around her does my whole world center
And meaning is her greatest gift to me.

The sight of her is beacon in the fog,
A great flame burning high to light my way.
My eyes cannot pass by her, though she be in a crowd
She draws me to her as bee is to his hive.

I'll not say she is beautiful, though others may.
The word cannot encompass her, she is Helene.
As far removed from other ladies fair
As the Sun is from the Moon.

To leave her is to lose my way.
I would I could go on without her as before,
But then I think upon my fate and know
My ship was lost until I found her light.

* * *

After I'd written my first half-dozen or so love poems from female perspectives, I found myself getting the urge to write one from a male perspective, because it would naturally be more like the medieval poems that I'd read up to that point than my female-perspective poems were. Writing from a viewpoint so different from my own was also a challenge that I wanted to take up, one that would prove (at least to me) that there was more to these poems than some unacknowledged love interest.

But what to write, what metaphor could I use that would sound appropriately masculine? I was slowly brainstorming ideas when I came across a medieval illumination (a hand-painted illustration in a medieval book) that showed a heavily-loaded boat out in the sea.

And suddenly, I knew what my main metaphor would be.

The earliest lighthouses were bonfires set at important points along the coast, like the mouth of a harbor or a dangerous headland. By the classical era, the most important of these bonfires were placed high up in towers, so they'd be visible from farther out to sea. They stayed pretty much the same until refractive glass and more powerful lamps changed the technology used in lighthouses. Even today, lighthouses help to keep boaters safe by showing them where they are.

That inspired a couple supplementary metaphors. Lodestone is a naturally-occurring magnet that's been used to make compasses since the Classical era and which were vital for shipboard navigation. And if we're talking about navigation, bees have the incredible ability to fly here and there for miles and still find their way home. During the Elizabethan era (and probably for a long time before and after that time), people believed that male bees were the ones who left the hive to go explore.

But no masculine love poem would be complete without mentioning his lady's beauty, and I took a bit of inspiration from Shakespeare for this part – though I went with hyperbole instead of the understated touch he took in "Sonnet 130." The only suitable lady to compare my sailor's love with is Helen of Troy, whose face is said to have launched a thousand ships in her husband's attempt to retrieve her.

I like to imagine that the poet who wrote this poem is Philippe from "A Sister's Lament." He seems to have written it sometime before he left home to join the Third Crusade.

Phyllis 20

While some men grow verbose
With admiration of the face and hair,
And some the forms and all the eyes
Of those fair maids they choose to love.

To write of love, I must see more
Than transitory gifts like these.
Erato bids me write of greater gifts
That worldly men do often overlook.

My lady's words a font of wisdom are,
Yet sweet her speech; she's never proud
Though she has cause to be.
These virtues from her matchless faith do grow.

And if my pen were equal to her grace,
Then even Time itself could not touch her.

* * *

In one of my college classes on British literature, we studied the sonnets of Thomas Lodge, a contemporary of Shakespeare's who published a book of his work entitled *Phillis Honored with Pastorall Sonnets, Elegies, and Amorous Delights* (now generally simplified to *Sonnets to Phillis*). For an assignment later that semester in which we were to explain a poem we hadn't studied in class, I chose "Sonnet XX." The professor let us be creative in our explanations, and I chose to re-write it in modern terms.

But some of the modern verbiage, while going over really well with my prof and classmates, just seemed too modern for the tone and theme of the poem. So I re-wrote the parts that bothered me, making an intermediate poem.

Lodge – and therefore I – wrote a sonnet in which the first quatrain (the first four lines) discusses those aspects of their lady-loves that other poets tend to write about. In the second quatrain, he says he needs more to awaken his muse. In the third, he talks about the muse-worthy qualities his lady has, ones that he considers more important than the other ladies' temporal graces. Lodge closes with a couplet in which he says that time could never overcome "her glories" if his style – which might mean style in the sense we now use it (as his use of it in line 6 clearly is) but which could also be a poetic contraction of "stylus," a medieval word for "pen" – were as wonderful as she is. He claims his skill isn't up to truly showcasing and immortalizing her beauty and other virtues, but I think time has shown that the poet underestimated himself in this regard. I can only hope my version or some of my other works have such staying power.

The word "not" in the final line of my "Phyllis" was originally "never." While I prefer the sense of "never," the final couplet was just one beat off from being in perfect iambic pentameter. I love it when that happens; reading iambs is like listening to your own heartbeat and iambic pentameter has been considered a perfect poetic form since at least Shakespeare's time. The temptation to close the poem with per-fection was greater than my desire to maximize the permanence of that negative statement.

Sonnet XX

Some praise the looks, and others praise the locks,
Of their fair queens, in love with curious words:
Some laud the breast where love his treasure locks
All like the eye that life and love affords.
But none of these frail beauties and unstable
Shall make my pen riot in pompous style;
More greater gifts shall my grave muse enable,
Whereat severer brows shall never smile.
I praise her honey-sweeter eloquence,
Which from the fountain of true wisdom floweth,
Her modest mien that matcheth excellence,
Her matchless faith which from her virtue growth;
And could my style her happy virtues equal,
Time had no power her glories to enthral.

Thomas Lodge, 1593

Though All the World May
be a Stage

Though all the world may be a stage
And all of us but actors on it,
I'll tread the boards I have to tread with you,
Say all my lines with feeling, just for you,
And pray our scenes be long together.

* * *

In one of the most famous soliloquies in all of Shakespeare's works, the character Jaques in *As You Like It* likens the stages of a man's life to a play, where each man plays seven different roles in turn as he passes slowly from infancy to old age.

The speaker in my poem assumes that the Bard is probably correct that the whole world is a stage where she has no control over her scenes or what lines she's supposed to say, she has decided to take control over how she says them and who she says them to.

Whether you look at her decision in terms of the conflict between the principles of predestination and free will or you see her in literary terms as someone written to be a passive principle who makes herself an active one, her decision to love and to express her love has made her a real person.

"The Seven Ages of Man"

All the world's a stage,
And all the men and women merely players;
They have their exits and their entrances;
And one man in his time plays many parts,
His acts being seven ages. At first the infant,
Mewling and puking in the nurse's arms;
And then the whining school-boy, with his satchel
And shining morning face, creeping like snail
Unwillingly to school. And then the lover,
Sighing like furnace, with a woeful ballad
Made to his mistress' eyebrow. Then a soldier,
Full of strange oaths, and bearded like the pard,
Jealous in honour, sudden and quick in quarrel,
Seeking the bubble reputation
Even in the cannon's mouth. And then the justice,
In fair round belly with good capon lin'd,
With eyes severe and beard of formal cut,
Full of wise saws and modern instances;
And so he plays his part. The sixth age shifts
Into the lean and slipper'd pantaloon,
With spectacles on nose and pouch on side;
His youthful hose, well sav'd, a world too wide
For his shrunk shank...

William Shakespeare, 1599

My Love's Reply to the Passionate Shepherd

Oh, sweet man, don't make for me
Promises that you cannot keep.
Tell me instead your love for me
Is deeper than the deepest river pool,
That it will last while rivers flow.
Tell me your love will warm me like a fire
While round us blow the coldest winter winds.
Say that your love will see us through those times
When we eat grasses with our sheep.
Show me your love is deep and true –
Why then, I may just love you too!

* * *

Once upon a time, Christopher Marlowe was the most famous poet and playwright of the Elizabethan era. Even before he'd graduated from Cambridge, he'd translated a book of Ovid's poetry from Latin into English. In the six years between then and his unsolved murder, he wrote five plays that were the blockbusters of his time and a small number of poems.

"The Passionate Shepherd to His Love" is Marlowe's most famous and influential poem, an Arcadian pastorale set in a world influenced by Classical literature and fantasies of bucolic peasant life. It inspired numerous poetic replies, most notably one by Sir Walter Raleigh where the nymph replies that his promises could move her to love if only the world were as bucolically timeless as his promises make it sound – so maybe "The Passionate Shepherd to His Love" is less an Arcadian pastorale than a poem in which the speaker lives in the real world but sees Arcadia through his rose-colored glasses.

I loved the thought of one poem being answered with another, but I didn't really like Raleigh's reply. I wanted to give the shepherd's lady-love a reply that didn't seem so cold, one that wouldn't break his heart. My shepherdess loves his promises and the love that she knows is behind them, but she's earthy enough to know that they live in the real world, not in Arcadia. She wants to replace his lofty promises with ones that have real meaning in their lives.

Whenever I do a poetry reading of this work, I always read the last two lines with enough of a flirtatious pop to make it clear that she loves him too, she just wants their future happiness together to be based on something more dependable than riverside performances from unusually-talented birds and being able to afford golden buckles on a shepherd's salary.

The Passionate Shepherd to His Love

Come live with me and be my love,
And we will all the pleasures prove
That valleys, groves, hills, and fields,
Woods, or steepy mountain yields.

And we will sit upon the rocks,
Seeing the shepherds feed their flocks,
By shallow rivers to whose falls
Melodious birds sing madrigals.

And I will make thee beds of roses
And a thousand fragrant posies,
A cap of flowers, and a kirtle
Embroidered all with leaves of myrtle;

A gown made of the finest wool
Which from our pretty lambs we pull;
Fair linèd slippers for the cold,
With buckles of the purest gold;

A belt of straw and ivy buds,
With coral clasps and amber studs:
And if these pleasures may thee move,
Come live with me, and be my love.

The shepherd swains shall dance and sing
For thy delight each May morning:
If these delights thy mind may move,
Then live with me and be my love.

Christopher Marlowe, 1588

I Beg Only For the Joy

I beg only for the joy of soft nights
Spent in the arms of him whom I love.
I beg only for the joy of sweet looks
Shared at each passing in a day.
Do not take these from your lady
Just for my protection!

Once waked, the need for your sweet touch
Overwhelms all thought of peace or safety.
I would flee with you as Yseult did
Into the woods to live with her sweet Tristan.
Protection means nothing to me anymore
If it means my heart must break for want of you.

My heart thinks back with longing
To those days when you first sought me.
Your lady could not think it true
That you would choose to stoop on such as I.
With each fleeting absence I would doubt,
And every look between us made doubts flee.

You reached for me in love, and first I thought it friendship.
Yet I was glad enough for even that.
You slipped your hand in mine and my heart raced.
I gasped with joy at the perfection of its fit.

You laid against me and I was minded of my brothers,
Yet the feelings thus engendered spoke nothing of fraternity.

The season of spring festivals brought with it
Evenings of bonfires and dancing in clear moonlight.
At dance, our hands slipped secretly together,
And long walks took us far from pryers' eyes.
T'was here that first we kissed 'neath orchard blooms –
Your kisses made my lips so very red!

Summer had come when first you led me to a secret space;
My yearning grew with every desperate touch.
My very breath returned to me through you,
Sweetened and heated, filling all my being.
If the fire it ignited truly was of Hell,
Then when I die, I'll feel a martyr's joy.

Those sweetest days too short were cut
By pryers who I think did envy me your love.
I knew that I had not the strength for this;
I could not act as if I did save that you do so well.
I cannot breathe, or eat, or sleep for want of you,
While moments with you only make those other times the worse.

If it must be love with you, or honour without,
I fear that honour cannot hold me.
My arms are empty with you not in them
And the ache would break my heart.
Reach for me again, and let me show you
How much sweeter passion is than pining distance.

* * *

When I first wrote this poem, I thought I'd have to be very careful about who read it, because the wrong people might read it and wrongly assume that it was based on my own experiences. I'd have to self-censor to protect myself – not a pleasant thought for an author! I eventually showed it to a few close friends, who thought it was safe and tended to think I was asking if it was too sexually explicit.

The first stanza of this poem sets the scene, mentioning two of the most wonderful physical expressions of love that I've found mentioned anywhere in the literature of the era. Of course, it hints of the conflict to come, when the lover might need to distance himself from his lady to protect her.

The Yseult and Tristan mentioned in the second stanza are two of the most famous lovers of the Middle Ages. The earliest stories about them are believed to be older than even the oldest tales of King Arthur, though they were eventually brought into his court due to their popularity during the twelfth and thirteenth centuries.

Tristan is the nephew of King Mark of Cornwall and is sent to Ireland to fetch Yseult, an Irish princess who was supposed to marry his uncle and thereby make peace between their peoples. Yseult's mother made a potion for Yseult to drink with Mark after their wedding that was supposed to make them fall deeply in love with one another, but the two young people accidentally find the bottle on their way back to Cornwall and share it with each other, thinking it was regular wine. They fall madly in love, but Yseult still has to marry Tristan's uncle. After spending several years trying to deny their love or simply keep it secret (and almost getting caught a few times), they run off and live together in the woods for seven years. Eventually, the call of duty makes them return to King Mark, but Tristan can't stand the situation and decides he must leave for Brittany. There, he encounters another Yseult and her royal father, who discovers that Tristan is sighing over someone named Yseult and is pleased to assume that his daughter is the girl Tristan is in love with. Tristan is wounded in battle in service to this king and, dying, sends for his Yseult, but the other one makes him believe she has refused to come. He dies of his wounds and lost hope, just before his Yseult arrives and dies in his arms.

Interestingly, the influential version of their story written by Gottfried von Strassburg in the early thirteenth century shows clear signs that he wrote it as an allegory for the alchemical process of refining the Philosopher's Stone from base elements, as I discuss in my article on Strassburg's *Tristan* (2016). This stone, also called the Fifth Element, was believed to perfect everything it touched, making Earth more like Heaven. Both the Philosopher's Stone and the Fifth Element have recently appeared in popular culture, giving the books and movies that use them an alchemical subtext that this particular history nerd, at least, finds intriguing.

But we move on in the third stanza to a hunting metaphor in which the lover is compared to a falcon, stooping on the lady he has chosen as his prey. Hunting with falcons and other birds of prey was a popular pastime among medieval nobility, one that even women could participate in and which could easily be used to represent the process of choosing and claiming one's beloved. In the rest of this stanza and all of the fourth, I wrote of likely early stages in their courtship, as told from the lady's perspective.

Events get a little heated in the fifth and sixth stanzas, where I borrowed heavily from some of the steamiest literature of the twelfth and thirteenth centuries. The fifth stanza is the last stage of the lovers' courtship, while the sixth is the stage that sells romance novels.

Unfortunately, courtly love was seldom between husband and wife, it was even argued that love between husband and wife was impossible because they were already bound by ties of duty. Theirs was most likely a political marriage, with a younger woman married to an older man, like Yseult and Mark. His younger knights would vie for her affections in an odd way of honoring him. But if they let themselves get carried away by passion beyond the pretty game that they were playing – which, if we're to believe the literature, happened fairly regularly – they were actually being disloyal to him. Not surprisingly, the church took a negative stance on the whole thing. Human nature hasn't changed in thousands of years, and our natural tendency is for us to move rather abruptly and without much thought from stanza five to stanza six.

The lady is aware that their love is a sin, but she can't regret it. The heat of their passion may be a foretaste of the fires of hell, but she desires it even while she recognizes the wages of their sin. Martyrs, on the other hand, were thought to be granted a taste of Paradise in the moments before their deaths, as a foretaste of the joys that awaited them in Heaven.

Being discovered would spell disaster for any lovers who had let their affair stray into the danger zone of stanza six. Nosy gossips, known in Provençal poetry as "lauzengiers" or "prying eyes" would talk of the couple. They might even do as Mordred did in Arthurian legends and bring the affair to the attention of the lady's husband, who would be an even more real threat than the gossips. These dangers have led the lovers to break off their affair in stanza seven, despite the pain this entails.

But in stanza eight, the lady declares her decision to choose love over safety. We can only hope that her beloved loves her as much as Tristan loved Yseult and that they have more time together than those two famous lovers did.

A Thing of Great Beauty and Virtue

A thing of great beauty and virtue
Is the treasure I keep from all men.
The box that contains it is covered in gold
But the rose inside puts it to shame.

This thing is a rose far too fair for the sun;
Its petals blush pink as a maiden's fair cheek.
The bee that finds its sweet centre
Will come away covered in nectar.

This thing is a prize I don't give away lightly,
For the man who wins it should be envied by all.
And if he despise it, I'll take it right back,
For this treasure is mine to bestow.

* * *

Folk of the Middle Ages were a racy sort, but generally not blatantly so. Between metaphor and oblique references, they could create poetry that was incredibly heated but wouldn't seem so unless the audience knew what they meant or was already inclined to read things into the work. I'm told that rock music of the 1970s and 80s is similar to medieval poetry in this respect, though I've done far less research on that subject and generally find it less interesting than medieval poetry. To each his or her own, as they say.

One popular oblique reference in medieval literature was the use of the French word "chose," meaning "thing," to speak of a lady's most private... well, you know.

In a burst of daring that might have had something to do with the lateness of the hour, I decided to create this poem. I found I needed to use metaphor to describe this "thing," and chose that of the rose, which Jean Renart used quite well in his turn-of-the-thirteenth-century lai, *Le Roman de la Rose* (not the *Roman de la Rose* by Guillaume de Lorris and Jean de Meung, the better and less famous one). In it, the rose is used metaphorically to represent the most beautiful lady in the kingdom, the rose-shaped birthmark on her thigh (used euphemistically, at least during the eighteenth and nineteenth centuries for a part of the female anatomy just north of the thigh), and her – again, you know. That part that's euphemized as "thigh." The bad guy almost ruins the lady, simply by claiming to have seen her rose when he hasn't even met her and doesn't recognize her when she comes to court to prove her innocence. I appreciated the way the signifier could refer to any or all of the associated signifieds, though of course sometimes it only makes sense for it to apply to the most risqué one.

If you remember from an earlier poem, bees were thought to be male, at least during Elizabethan times.

The Lady Whom I See

The lady whom I see reflected in your eyes
Is one whom any man would fight to claim.
Her form more fair than Helene in Troy,
Her heart is gentle beyond measure,
She has no peer in any court.

The sun looks lovingly upon her
And warms her with his gentle kiss.
The moon shines brightly every night
That she may never lose her way.
The brightest star is dark beside her.

I do not know which it may be that I fear more –
That she might one day be gone from your eyes
Or that I see her image in another's.
My greatest desire is to be her for you,
And when I look in your eyes, I am.

* * *

When we love someone, we often have that person's faults minimized in our eyes and their strengths magnified. Add to that the self-esteem issues that many of us have, and the difference between how a person sees herself and how her lover sees her can be dramatic. And yet, love is magic. When she looks in her lover's eyes and sees herself as he sees her, she believes – even if his vision of her is somewhat hyperbolic. As far as her lover is concerned, the lady even puts Helen of Troy to shame and is so wonderful that everything on or above the earth is also in love with her.

But that could also be a problem, not just because she fears the loss of his love. A second would-be lover would complicate her position dramatically, even if nothing happened. She doesn't want that, she only wants to remain her lover's impossibly-perfect lady.

The Unnamed Lady

The lady whom I have never the right to name
Given by Heaven to gift us with grace
Each word of hers brings wisdom, joy, and peace
With every step, she frees the soul to sing.
She strolls the garden, roses turn away,
Embarrassed that their beauty is compared with hers.
She sings and all the songbirds stop to listen.
She dances, and angels seek to join her.

But all of us below are now made fools by grief.
The birds will never sing again, clouds weep great tears.
The roses drop their red and scented robes.
For God has called his most perfect angel
To rejoin His eternal heavenly chorus.
And I must suffer here until He calls my name.

* * *

My studies of sixteenth and seventeenth century French sonnets inspired me to try my hand at one, which I originally wrote in French and only translated into English so my friends could understand it. It rhymes in French, though not much in English.

French sonnets are divided into an octave consisting of eight lines or two quatrains of four lines each, followed by a sestet consisting of a third quatrain and a couplet. The first eight lines set up a situation, followed by an abrupt change known as a volta that leads the reader into a contrasting situation in the sestet. In French "alexandrine" sonnets, the rhythm is iambic hexameter, with two more syllables than the iambic pentameter we learned about when studying Shakespeare. A complex rhyme scheme ties the ends of the lines together, and the lines themselves might be divided by a cæsura in the middle of each line.

In my poem, the speaker may wax slightly hyperbolic when he speaks of the great beauty of his lady, whom he feels unworthy even to name. Everything she does is a blessing to those around her. She makes the most beautiful flowers in the garden hang their heads in shame to be compared with her. In an intentional reference to the biblical tale of women so beautiful that angels came to Earth to reproduce with them, her dancing makes angels want to partner her on the dance floor and possibly elsewhere.

Then comes the volta. Everyone who relished her beauty and grace weeps now, for the lady has died. In a world where plagues – now known as epidemics – could kill off more than half the population in a handful of years and where an estimated one in six pregnancies resulted in the death of the mother, the baby, or both, such an event would not be unlikely. The death of a beloved is a common trope in literature from this era and right through the early twentieth century, when medical advances started to significantly affect mortality rates. The lover's one small comfort is that the lady has gone back to being an angel in heaven, where he may someday join her.

La dame qui

La dame qui je n'ai jamais le droit d'appeler,
Donnée par le ciel pour nous amèner la grâce.
Chaque mot porte la sagesse, la joie, et la paix,
Chaque pas de lui libère l'âme pour chanter.
Elle se promène pour l'aire, et les roses se détournent
Parce qu'on les a comparées avec son soleil.
Elle chante et tous les oiseaux tendront l'oreille.
Elle danse et les anges luttent pour prendre un tour.

Mais tous de nous ici-bas sont fous de chagrin.
Les oiseaux ne chantent jamais encore, les nuages pleurent,
Les roses détruisent leurs robes parfumées et pourpres.
Le dieu a récupéré son plus parfait ange
Pour rejoindre son chœur céleste et éternel.
Je dois souffrir ici-bas jusqu'à Il m'appelle.

Sophie G. Michaels, 2013

Sanguine Man

Born of flame near-purified,
Your fire brings to life
All those you touch.

With ruddy skin and cheerful mien,
You radiate your energy like heat.
A man of gold, confident.

Flamboyant and vivacious,
Shakespeare's greatest actor
Back to tread the boards.

Courageous 'gainst flame or foe,
As eager to encounter them as he could be
In love of woman or the feast.

Brave warlord and high king,
Bold and decisive leader of men,
Regal in speech and bearing.

A man who spent his life
Always reaching with both hands
For each experience that life could bring.

Go now, and reunite
With the Heavenly Spirit
That gave to you the life you've shared.

* * *

When I thought that this book was ready for publication, a dear older friend died suddenly. This man was both a firefighter and a legend in the reenactment community, chosen older brother of my beloved. I had to write something for him, but my muse was grieving as much as the rest of us.

As one friend after another rose to speak about this pillar of his communities, I was struck by the imagery that kept cropping up, which reminded me of the language used to refer to Juliet in Shakespeare's play about her and Romeo. I had written an article a few years ago in which I explored the play as an allegory for the most important alchemical process, which used the lovers' deaths to bring heaven to earth.

But the reason I had originally noticed this allegory was the constant use of imagery that humoral theory linked to the sun whenever Shakespeare was referring to Juliet. You can think of at least one example of this, probably more. And these same words – along with others I'd come across in my research – kept cropping up in people's memories of Dan. It felt strangely appropriate.

Medieval people still believed in the four "elements" that were first theorized around 450 BC, which was the basis of the humoral theory of Hippocrates and Galen. According to this theory, everything on Earth was composed of some combination of the four elements of earth, air, fire, and water. These four elements were the basis of the four humors – blood, phlegm, black bile, and yellow bile. These four liquids flow through our bodies and, according to Galen, determine our health by how well they are balanced. People's personalities were determined by which humor held precedence, and different balances were considered more suitable for different people depending on whether they were young or old, male or female. A person with a sanguine personality is ruled by their blood, which is composed primarily of air (don't ask). This made their temperaments wet and hot (like Florida). It was considered to be the usual temperament for young men.

Before you decide that humoral theory is an absurd relic of pre-scientific thinking, consider that George Washington's death in 1799 came about because he contracted a cold that developed into a sore and swollen throat. His doctors bled him, which today makes some people wonder if excessive bleeding contributed to his death by making it harder for his body to fight off the infection in his throat. And this was only 224 years ago, a fraction of the nearly 2000 years since Galen theorized about the four humors. Even more recently, humoral theory served as the basis for most of the early psychological theories, and its terminology continues to crop up in psychological texts.

Dan, like Juliet, was sanguine, ruled by the sun and bringing life to whatever he touched. I've tried to reflect some small portion of his sanguinity here.

6

Higher Loves

Six Days

"Let's start with light," One thinks,
And instant bursts a light so bright
That only One could see it without pain,
If any else were there. One reaches out,
Forms eddies in the light, and smiles.

One touches a small eddy, feels it spin
Tighter, grow dense and round,
Brighten like the greater stars.
Fingers vibrate as its outer disk
Ripples and twists with shifting rocks.

Another day, the rocks have grown.
"Cool down a bit," One tells them,
"I've plans for you."
The sizzling stops, their surface goes
From red and orange to black.

And then, another day, to green.
The surface listens for the One
To tell it what is next.
"Yes," One says. "More of this,
More growth, more everywhere."

"Closer," One says another day,
And Life begins to fly and walk and swim.
"Closer!" One shouts, and flies
And swims among the life created.
One walks through field and forest.

"We're almost there," One says,
Trailing fingers through a bit of clay.
Water flows along behind, and at One touch,
Life breathes and looks upon the One
With eyes reflecting love.

* * *

It often seems like we're forced to decide whether we're going to look at the world through the lens of religion or science. But while science speaks the language of the mind, religion speaks to the soul. We need them both. I realized that the first time I read JRR Tolkien's *The Silmarillion*, which begins with the most beautiful, most lyrical prose interpretation of the first chapter of Genesis you'll ever read anywhere. While science has always made more sense to me than the religious teaching I received as a child, I needed this beauty in my life. My soul sang out that it was true, in all but perhaps the most literal sense.

And then I realized that the key to bringing the two together was spelled out in straightforward language, not once but twice in the *Bible*, first in Psalms and then in Second Peter. God, being immortal and eternal, has a different sense of time than we do. A thousand years is an incredibly long time to us, but to God it's the equivalent of a day – less than a day, a watch in the night. It's just one little overnight shift.

If there's no difference to God between a millennium and a night shift, then what difference is there between a day and a million years? A billion?

Not to call God an unreliable narrator, but... let's just say His point of view is rather different from ours. And that first chapter of Genesis is entirely through His point of view. It's not like there was anyone else around at the time who could have narrated the story to humans later on. And of course those humans He told the story to assumed they understood it better than they did, because we humans are really good at making that kind of assumption.

So six days, six billion years, what's the difference? Give me a minute to think about it...

Following my own possibly-incorrect assumptions, I laid out the stages of Creation from the Big Bang onward in this poem, separating events into the familiar six days. For the first five days, I followed the scientific interpretation of the events involved, stepping into the Biblical/metaphorical only for the last day, when the One creates humanity. The Biblical interpretation seems to better fit the joy and love permeating the entire process than a description of evolution in human terms possibly could, and of course it fits better in one short stanza. But perhaps they are just two different ways of looking at the same thing, at least in the timescale of the One.

For love is the purpose of Creation, love and the joy of creating new things. The One takes intense pleasure in each new stage of Creation but is essentially alone until the final stage, when the first humans look back at the One. And here, I finally had a mirror capable of showing the whole purpose of Creation. Literature provides us with numerous examples of times when the eyes are described metaphorically as either windows or mirrors. This metaphor allowed me to overtly mention the One's love of all Creation without metaphorically burning out our retinas by looking directly at the source.

Artemis

Men call her man-hater, bitch, and worse,
But they cannot see her,
Will not understand her.
She is not of their world.

Sought by many who would take her,
Own her,
Master her;
Men who see her only as
The hunter's greatest prize,
She flees them in anger.

Betrayed,
Tricked into slaying
The only man who could
Ever be her true companion
And her love,
She flees the memory
Of that great loss.

She will give herself only
To those who give themselves to her.
She will run wild in the forests
And dance in silver moonlight,
Giving herself only
To those who share her soul.
She is the Virgin Unassailable
And men seek her at their peril.

* * *

Artemis is the wildest and most primordial of the ancient Greek goddesses, the one whose character was set before the Greeks became civilized folk who lived in cities. One of only two virgin goddesses in the Greek pantheon, she lives in the wild, attended only by other female hunters and the wild animals that are more a part of her world than the men and women of the cities are.

Artemis defends her privacy jealously but not without mercy. The most famous example of this happens when young prince Aktaion of Thebes spies on her as she bathes in a shady river pool. So he would never be able to tell anyone that he'd seen her naked, she turns him into a stag. Of course, his hunting dogs chase after him, take him down, and tear him to pieces. But when young Sipriotes accidentally comes across her while she's bathing, she just transforms him into a girl. I wonder if he sticks around with Artemis' other female followers after that.

There was one man who was worthy of her, one who got along with her so well that they were talking about marriage. This is where their story took a tragic turn, for when Orion the hunter mentioned their upcoming nuptials to Artemis' twin brother Apollo, he got jealous. For hundreds of years, it had been just the two of them against anyone who offended them or their mother Leto, a human woman who'd been one of Zeus' temporary loves. And now he was losing her to – gasp! – a mortal man, even if he was a big one.

Apollo let his jealousy get the better of him. He turned to trickery, convincing Orion to walk out into the depths of the sea, to show off how big and sturdy he was (I never said Orion was a genius). Then he got Artemis to show off what a good shot she was, by aiming at that tiny little island way out on the horizon. She hit it, of course. She wanted to show Orion what a good shot she was, but he was nowhere to be seen. And then, a few days later, his body washed up on shore with one of her arrows sticking out of his head.

Suddenly realizing she'd been tricked by one of the only two men in her life into killing the other, she took off into the wild mountains, trying to get away from any reminder of her great loss. Is it any wonder that she swore off men so completely?

I am Persephone

I am Persephone,
Nature's Child, Death's Queen, Reborn One,
Dancing again for love of life,
Basking in the sweet rays of Apollo's love,
And loving him again as Nature must.

Yet Autumn comes, and with it Hades.
This time he speaks soft words, makes kindly promises.
He will raze the roof from off his lands
And make them fair as any of Apollo's.

I am Persephone, and I am torn.
For I would never leave Apollo's lands,
But Duty bids me give my King his due
And Hope whispers that he might speak truth.
But if I choose to go with him, I never can return.

* * *

The story of Demeter and her daughter Persephone is one of the first Greek myths I remember reading, though I'd already read Homer and Virgil and had presumably read enough Greek mythology somewhere to understand those larger works. It feels like I've always known the Greek myths, and perhaps I have.

Persephone's story really struck me, back when I first read it. Here was a girl, not much older than I was at the time, the daughter of the goddess of all flowering and fruiting plants and niece of the most powerful god in the Greek pantheon. The entire world was basically her mother's garden, a veritable Garden of Eden, and Persephone has full run of this beautiful place.

Then one day, when she was out picking flowers, the ground split open and a fearsome-looking old man in a chariot drawn by four skeletal black horses came bursting up out of the ground. Before she could move, he grabbed her and drove the chariot back underground, making her drop her flowers. Everything around the hole in the ground died in the instant he appeared, and for the first time death appears in our world.

Demeter was the original mama bear, or maybe she's just based on the original mama bears. She has the dreadful feeling that her daughter's disappearance might have something to do with that weird dead spot in her garden, but she has to conduct her own investigation and it takes her months to find out anything more. While she's searching, she doesn't have the time or attention to tend her garden. By the time she has the evidence to go to her brother Zeus and tell him that their brother Hades has kidnapped her daughter and must be made to give her back, the people of the Earth are all crying out to Zeus and the other deities to save them from the death by starvation that they all face if Demeter doesn't go back to tending her garden. Zeus asks Demeter what would satisfy her, but he surely already knows.

Zeus sends Hermes to order Hades to release the girl, but Hades still has a trick up his sleeve. He pretends to be willing to obey his brother, reminding Persephone that hospitality was a cornerstone of Greek culture and asking her to have a bite or two of the food from his table before she leaves, to show there are no hard feelings between them.

Persephone had sat beside Hades on the dais in the cold, dark kingdom of the dead, growing pale and wan as she refused to eat in a hunger strike that would have melted any heart that wasn't as cold and dead as Hades' was. But now, eager to do and say anything to get away, she picks up a pomegranate that had been split open and loosens a few tiny arils from one side, popping them into her mouth as she rises to leave.

The pomegranate should have been a safe choice. It was one of her mother's fruits, and it has a long history of representing fertility because of the hundreds of seeds in it, each separately packaged in a beautiful garnet-red juice packet called an aril. Fertility, even science tells us, is one of the central characteristics of life.

But, as Hades – or maybe Hermes, who had been too startled to stop her in time – reminds her, the food of the dead is only for the dead. By eating even a tiny bite of it, she has accepted her place in the kingdom of the dead.

Demeter wasn't willing to accept that, and Zeus couldn't afford to make her. Unless she went back to tending her garden, everyone in the world would die, and then the gods themselves would become powerless. So he comes up with a compromise that satisfies nobody completely. Since Persephone had eaten three (maybe four) arils, she would spend that many months down in the Underworld, as Hades' queen. The rest of the year, she would spend above ground, in the world of the living. People would grow and harvest enough food in the eight or nine months of the year that Persephone was at home with her mother to get them through the three or four months when she was in the underworld and Demeter mourned for her as for the dead.

Persephone's joy each time she returns to the land of the living is easy to understand. The soft, perfumed air of her mother's garden makes her want to dance, especially after the musty stillness of the underworld. The sun feels so good on her face, like a lover's kiss. The sun god Apollo, a much more appropriate lover for Persephone than Hades could ever be, must surely love this beautiful young woman.

But she is also a wife, if only during those cold, dark months of winter. I imagined that one year Hades actually seemed to care that he was killing her by making her spend any time at all in the underworld with him. He comes to her when she's above ground, promising to change his ways, change everything about his kingdom and himself. He will out-Apollo the sun god himself. He will become a good husband, if only she decides to come home with him.

He's lying. We know it, she knows it, he might even know it. But in the world of the ancient Greeks, does that give her the right to ignore her "duty" and seek life and love? All she knows is that she'll have to live or die with whatever decision she makes, for eternity.

Perfection

In eastern lands, they say,
Each craftsman must
Before he's done each piece
Add one small intended flaw
That he not offend his God,
The only Perfect Craftsman.

Yet is it not the greater offense
To dare believe that this
One small intended flaw
Could the subtle difference be
Between one's own work
And that of God?

* * *

On my first trip to Spain, I did what every good medievalist does and visited every castle, cathedral, and other structure I could find that was at least a couple centuries old. At one such palace, where I was enjoying a spread of rooms built off an arcaded central garden and admiring a stone wall with intricate carving all over it that turned it into stone filigree, the tour guide mentioned that Muslim artisans of the era were required to add some intentional flaw to each of their works, so as to not offend God.

I loved the idea, even though the thinking seems – at least to me – to smell of hubris.

I could just see it. The poor artisan spends weeks, maybe even months or years carving these beautiful, detailed carvings where he's paid based on the volume of stone dust he creates in the carving process. He carefully makes his one small, intentional "mistake," probably someplace where you'd have to climb up on a ladder and look closely to see it, because that's how we as humans deal with that kind of a requirement.

Then, as he gets down off his scaffold and starts to clear away his tools, he sees it.

The big mistake.

He'd made that unintentional mistake so early in the process that it affected *everything* he did afterwards, making the entire panel a mistake. Everyone will see it, at least if they have half a clue about what he was supposed to carve. In his mind, *everyone* has at least half a clue.

Because that's how things go for us mere mortals. Our job is often figuring out how to turn our big mistakes into something beautiful. Often, the only way to salvage them is to ask for help from the only Perfect Craftsman.

7

Love Continues

I've Slipped the Surly Bonds of Earth

I've slipped the surly bonds of Earth
and sailed on Heaven's tides,
I've danced with angels, stars, and gods
in realms where none have trod.
The Earth is not my master, nor am I his slave.
For I have strode the skyways
and will not be caught again.

* * *

I wrote this poem shortly after I left home at 18. I looked up one beautiful fall day to see a small plane doing cartwheels and other aerial maneuvers that seemed to prove that the pilot felt the same exhilaration of newfound freedom that I felt that day. The poem came to me within moments.

The odd thing is, while I didn't realize it at the time, I was borrowing the first line from a speech President Reagan gave in 1986, just after the *Challenger* disaster. Speaking of the seven astronauts who tragically lost their lives that day, he said, "We shall never forget them nor the last time we saw them, as they prepared for their mission and waved good-bye and slipped the surly bonds of Earth to touch the face of God." This line clearly made a big impact on me when I first heard it.

But as great a communicator as Reagan was, he didn't come up with that line on his own. He was quoting a World War II pilot named John Gillespie Magee, Jr., who went to England via Canada to fly missions over France and England in the RCAF. He wrote his famous poem, "High Flight," on 3 September 1941, just three months before he died at the age of 19. The theme and spirit of the poem seem to distract readers from the fact that it's a sonnet, written in iambic pentameter with a rhyme scheme of *abab cdcd efe gfg*. That's not easy, especially if you want to create a work with such a lightweight, joyful feel! Few of his other works survive, though he won awards for some of them during his short lifetime.

High Flight

Oh! I have slipped the surly bonds of Earth
And danced the skies on laughter-silvered wings;
Sunward I've climbed, and joined the tumbling mirth
Of sun-split clouds, — and done a hundred things
You have not dreamed of — wheeled and soared and swung
High in the sunlit silence. Hov'ring there,
I've chased the shouting wind along, and flung
My eager craft through footless halls of air...
Up, up the long, delirious burning blue
I've topped the wind-swept heights with easy grace
Where never lark, or ever eagle flew —
And, while with silent, lifting mind I've trod
The high untrespassed sanctity of space,
Put out my hand, and touched the face of God.

John Gillespie Magee, Jr., 1941

Luna's Lady

Luna's lady is a fairy blue,
Left behind by choice in her immortal
Fellows' exodus from Earth.
Desiring but to know the fate
Of this poor race they left to free.
Garbed in a gauze azure she is,
With silver pendants hanging.
And ev'ry day she goes
To stand upon the highest pinnacle of light
To watch the world below.
Ages pass, and at last
With waning hope she turns away,
Draping herself in deepest black
As three rise from that world
To meet the skies and free her.

* * *

What if the reason we don't see elves and fairies everywhere is because they left us at some point in our history? What if the reason they left is because they knew we would never grow up into a mature species unless they gave us some space to decide our own fate? What if they left us out of love for us and hope for what we could become?

And what if someone stayed behind, to keep watch?

The elf-lady who stays behind is immortal, but that doesn't save her from feelings of depression as her vigil appears increasingly pointless. She's in the process of leaving her post when the first lunar launch happens, signaling the beginning of a brighter era.

But does she see it in time, or does she give up?

The theme of this poem is the conflict between love and loneliness, hope and despair. The elves' love for us and hope for our future are the reason they leave us and why one of them stays on a centuries-long vigil. But such a long vigil is a lonely one, even for an immortal. With loneliness – and a period that boasted two World Wars and the inception of the Nuclear Age in less than half a century – the lady becomes depressed and eventually decides to give up. Her long vigil has been wasted; this species is about to destroy itself.

I intentionally left it unclear whether the lady sees the three astronauts who "*rise from that world / To meet the skies and free her*" or if she gives up just a moment too soon. You wouldn't think a moment could make such a vital difference to an immortal being!

I wrote this poem at age fifteen, when I'd been writing poetry for at least eight years (and no, you don't want to see my earliest works, unless you're my mom). This poem and one involving the personification of nature called "Marilynn's Mists" that I'd written a year earlier are presumably the earliest of my "adult" poems, chosen for publication by editors who'd had no idea I was still just a child. That realization thrilled me back then, as I hope it inspires other young poets today.

My Hidden Treasure

My heart was tossed about and broken
So many times times before I met you.
I glued it back together – oh, so many times –
I swear there was more glue than plate to it.

I learned that I must shelter it to keep it whole.
As soon as I learned how, I wrapped it well
In bubble film and packing paper,
Then set it in a box marked "fragile – do not touch."

I wondered in my youth why none I met did move me,
Why none could raise in me the love I yearned to feel.
No thoughts they spared to find my heart;
It was not in plain sight, and so it did not matter.

One day you came to me and told me I had treasures,
And if I let you look you'd give them back to me.
I doubted you but let you look – I don't know why.
At least while you were here I would not be alone.

You hunted many months until you found that box,
Then blew away the dust and showed it to me.
"Someone packed a treasure here, come see it!
If I could only see this every day, I'd be content!"

I knew right then that it was meant for you
And that you'd treasure it as priceless,
Though I could only see the cracks and glue.
I gave it to you in that instant, and myself as well.

* * *

What happens when you're living and breathing medieval courtly love poetry but you have to move for work? In my case, you write a poem that uses a broken plate and bubble film in an allegory about love. The contrast between the allegorical style and the quotidian items in it makes for a rich and unique poem that I particularly like.

In my mind's eye, the speaker lives in a house based on my dad's childhood home, so the box is hidden in a chest in a garret room in the upper attic, behind the huge chimney that almost hides the entrance to the room (the real version of this room is thought by historians to prove that the house really was a stop on the Underground Railroad). No wonder it takes her lover so long to find it!

I hadn't thought about it at the time, but the plate in this poem makes me think of the ancient Japanese art of *kintsugi*, or "gold repair." Layers of gold and lacquer are used to glue a broken ceramic back together, creating a piece of art that is arguably more beautiful and valuable than the unbroken original. A *kintsugi* heart has been broken and healed by its owner's experiences, making her stronger and better prepared to build a new love with someone else. Since anyone who loves will have a broken heart at some point, there's a *kintsugi* heart in each of us who've ever recovered from that first (or fifth) broken heart.

For Further Reading

Abelard, Peter & Heloise. *The Letters of Abelard and Heloise.* Translated by Betty Radice. Penguin Books, 1974.

Anonymous. *The Song of Roland: Chanson de Roland.* Translated by C. K. Scott Moncrieff, 1919.

Bar-sur-Aube, Bertrand de. *The Song of Girart of Vienne: A Twelfth-Century Chanson de Geste.* Translated by Michael A. Newth. Tempe: Arizona Center for Medieval and Renaissance Studies, 1999.

Cornualle, Heldris de. *Silence: A Thirteenth-Century French Romance.* A facing-page translation by Sarah Roche-Mahdi. East Lansing: Michigan State U P, 1992.

Joinville, Jean de. "The Life of Saint Louis." In *Joinville and Villehardouin: Chronicles of the Crusades.* Translated by M. R. B. Shaw. London & New York: Penguin Books, 1963.

Pizan, Christine de. *The Book of the City of Ladies.* Translated by Earl Jeffrey Richards. New York: Persea Books, 1982. Originally published as *Le Livre de la Cité des Dames,* c. 1405.

Renart, Jean. *The Romance of the Rose: or Guillaume de Dole.* Translated by Patricia Terry and Nancy Vine Durling. Philadelphia: U of Pennsylvania P, 1993.

Strassburg, Gottfried von. *Tristan with the 'Tristran' of Thomas.* Translated by Arthur Thomas Hatto. London & New York: Penguin Books, 1960.

About the Poet

Sophie G. Michaels was born in the rich rolling hills of southeastern Pennsylvania and has made her home in central Florida since her late teens, but her soul was born in the castles of medieval France. In her poetry and her fiction, she brings to life the people of this fascinating era.

Sophie's works have appeared in *Synergy*; *The Odds are Against Us*; *An Atlas to Time, Space, and Bonfires*; and a variety of journals and poetry anthologies. She can be found online at https://sophiegmichaelswrites.wordpress.com.